A Contribution To The Knowledge Of The Tunicates Of The Pribilof Islands

William Emerson Ritter

In the interest of creating a more extensive selection of rare historical book reprints, we have chosen to reproduce this title even though it may possibly have occasional imperfections such as missing and blurred pages, missing text, poor pictures, markings, dark backgrounds and other reproduction issues beyond our control. Because this work is culturally important, we have made it available as a part of our commitment to protecting, preserving and promoting the world's literature. Thank you for your understanding.

XIX.—A CONTRIBUTION TO THE KNOWLEDGE OF THE TUNICATA OF THE PRIBILOF ISLANDS.

By WILLIAM EMERSON RITTER, Ph. D.,
Associate Professor of Zoölogy, University of California.

The Tunicata here described reached me in two installments. The first was collected by President Jordan himself on Lukanin Beach, St. Paul Island, during July, 1896; the second by Messrs. R. E. Snodgrass, Trevor Kincaid, and A. W. Greeley from July to September, 1897. This second installment contains specimens gathered from various points, which will be found specified in connection with the descriptions of the species. The first lot contained four species, viz, *Dendrodoa tuberculata, D. subpedunculata, Aplidiopsis jordani,* and *Polyclinum globosum*. It is perhaps significant that the last two species are not represented in the second installment, even though this contains a much larger number of specimens all told and is the result of a considerably longer continued and wider range of collecting. President Jordan informs me that the summer of 1896 was particularly stormy at the Pribilofs. The following is a list of the species contained in the collection:

Ascidiae Simplices:
    Boltema elegans, Herdman.
    Styela greeleyi. New species.
    Dendrodoa tuberculata. New species.
        subpedunculata. New species.

Ascidiae Compositae:
    Polyclinum globosum. New species.
        pannosum. New species.
    Aplidiopsis jordani. New species.
    Amaroucium kincaidi. New species.
        pribilovense. New species.
        snodgrassi. New species.
    Synoicum irregulare. New species.

Facts of some interest relating to the geographical distribution are brought out by considering the species here described in connection with other known far northern tunicates. Of the genera represented, two, viz, *Dendrodoa* and *Synoicum,* are, so far as we now know, confined to the Arctic or North Atlantic oceans. Of the other species, *Boltenia elegans* is known only from the extreme North Pacific; *Aplidiopsis jordani* has as its nearest ally *A. sarsii,* Huitfeldt-Kaas, from Lofoten Islands; and both *Amaroucium pribilovense* and *A. snodgrassi* have apparently rather closer affinities with *A. mutabile*, Sars, from Hammerfest, than with any other species of the genus. It would thus seem that at least half of the species might be regarded as characteristically far northern; and the evidence at hand seems to justify the conclusion that there exists a distinct Arctic Ascidian fauna.

Before entering upon the main work in hand, I wish to express not only my satisfaction at having the opportunity to make this contribution to the knowledge of this group of animals, but also my pleasure at doing the work at the instance of one so watchful and energetic as President Jordan ever is in all his capacities as a promoter of learning. I also most gladly acknowledge the important assistance that has been rendered me in the work by one of my advanced students, Miss Edith Byxbee.

Dendrodoa tuberculata, new species.

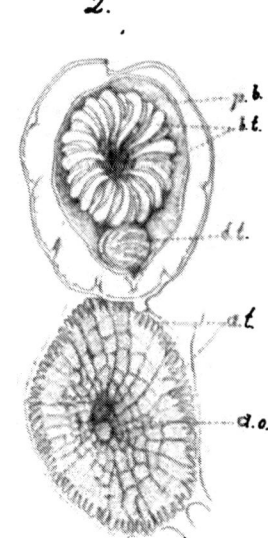

General characteristics.—Subcylindrical, about one-third longer than broad, quite regular in form, usually attached by the posterior end, sometimes by one side. Dimensions of a large specimen: Length, 53 mm.; greatest diameter, 35 mm. Entire surface closely beset with short, blunt, irregular tubercles. Color brown to yellowish brown, a little darker at the anterior end. (Fig. 1.)

Test.—Coriaceous, almost horny, scarcely 1 mm. thick excepting through the tubercles. Dull opaque white on cut surfaces; inner surface, after being separated from the mantle, with a somewhat pearly luster. Contains no vessels.

Mantle.—Well developed, considerably thicker than test, composed mostly of muscle fibers, most of which run lengthwise of the animal; some "mesenchyme" cells among the muscle fibers. An orange coloring matter in the mantle, some of which is contained in irregular branched bodies (crystals? excreted material?), and some diffused through the muscle fibers themselves.

Branchial apparatus.—No projecting siphons, orifices scarcely detectable, so completely are they hidden by the tubercles of the test. Both situated at anterior end, not far apart. Branchial tentacles simple, about 24 in number, not of equal length, but not regularly alternating, a long and a short one; the circle close to the peripharyngeal band. Atrial tentacles present, numerous, short, and small. Dorsal tubercle conspicuous, biscuit-shaped, the horseshoe-shaped mouth of the hypophysis situated on its surface. (Fig. 2 *d. t.*)

Branchial sac, figs. 3 and 4, with four longitudinal folds on each side, the pair nearest the dorsal lamina somewhat larger than the others, each of these having about 14 longitudinal vessels, while each of the others have about 10. Usually two or three longitudinal vessels between each two folds. Transverse vessels numerous, averaging

0.2 mm. apart; intermediate transverse vessels, i. e., vessels crossing the stigmata, frequently present, but small. About 20 stigmata in the space corresponding to the interval between two internal longitudinal vessels. The series of stigmatae extend fully to the dorsal lamina. (Fig. 3.)

Dorsal lamina a plane narrow membrane. "Endocarps" (fig. 5 *en'c.*) present, numerous, and rather large, contain many pigment cells.

Digestive tract.—Situated on left side of branchial sac, the portion posterior to the stomach forming an S, the two loops of which are closed; the end of the limb of the S corresponding to the pylorus is extended to form the stomach and œsophagus; the two last-mentioned parts of about equal length. Œsophagus issues from the dorsal side of the branchial sac. Stomach not well set off from intestine; considerably longer than broad, its walls with numerous internal folds, but smooth on outer surface; rectal portion of intestine runs close along the œsophagus, but extends farther forward than mouth of œsophagus.

Sexual organs.—On the right side of

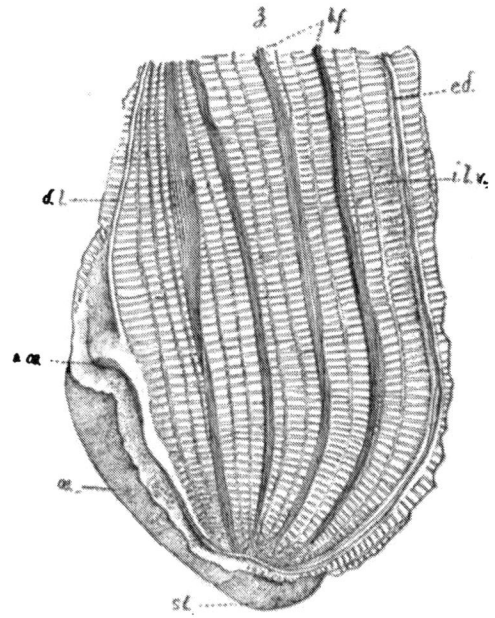
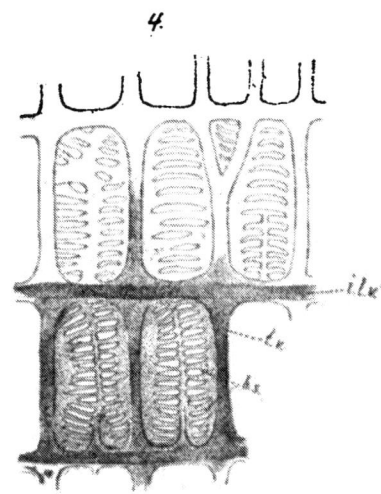

the animal only, closely attached to the inner surface of the mantle. Ovary (fig. 5, *ov.*), a long, branched, cylindrical body of uniform diameter throughout, the whole consisting of a basal portion situated near to and extending approximately parallel with the midventral line, and five or six simple branches given off from this basal piece, these reaching dorsalward and being inclined somewhat toward the anterior end of the animal.

This species clearly belongs to the genus *Dendrodoa*, founded by MacLeay, 1824, as a subgenus of Ascidia. His species was from Winter Island, in Fox Channel. Until now no other member of the genus has been described.

The chief differences between the present species and *D. glandaria*, MacLeay, are as follows:

The test of the latter is described as "whitish, subpellucid, coriaceous, and smooth;" and in another connection the author speaks of the ovary as being visible through the test. The "anterior nervous tubercle" (dorsal tubercle) in MacLeay's species is said to have "many spirals." These are undoubtedly the hypophysis mouth, which in our species, as shown by the description, is horseshoe shaped.

The "pharynx" of *D. glandaria* is described as being situated "at the bottom of the body cavity." By the "pharynx" is here evidently meant the entrance to the œsophagus; and this opening in our species, it will be observed, is on the dorsal side of the branchial sac. (Fig. 3, *o. œ.*)

In the structure of the branchial sac the two species differ in the number of longitudinal vessels between the folds, there being three and sometimes four in our species, while there are only two in MacLeay's species. It is thus seen that the two species are very distinct.

Herdman, 1882, has expressed the opinion that the genus *Dendrodoa* is not distinct from *Styela*. The genus is based on the position and character of the ovary, this being single, branched, and situated on the right side of the body here, while *Styela* has several unbranched ovaries situated on both sides of the body.

In his diagnosis of the genus *Styela*, written in 1882, Herdman speaks of the genitalia as being "in the form of one or more simple, lobed, or branched bodies." According to this definition *Dendrodoa* would, so far as this character is concerned, be merged in *Styela*. The same author has, however, in his Revised Classification of the Tunicata, 1891, stated that the gonads of *Styela* are present "on both sides of the body." As this is essentially the view of the case held by Savigny, 1816, MacLeay, 1824, Hancock, 1868, and Heller, 1877, and others who have written about the genus, it has seemed to me best to regard the difference as sufficiently great and constant to justify the recognition of both genera. I do not, however, believe that it is any more closely related to *Styela* than to *Polycarpa*, or any more closely related to *Styela* than the latter is to *Polycarpa*.[1] There are a large number of specimens in the collection, all from St. Paul Island.

Dendrodoa subpedunculata, new species.

General characteristics.—Subspherical; slightly elongated anteroposteriorly, frequently showing a tendency to be pedunculated; somewhat laterally compressed. Usually attached by the posterior end, and by only a small area, so that specimens may be more or less pendulous. Of the two dozen specimens at hand, 13 are attached close together on a small bit of seaweed, indicating an aggregated habit for the species (fig. 7). In one instance two individuals were fused together by their tests (fig. 7 a). Length from 1 to 1.5 cm.; surface rather closely but

---

[1] Kiær, 1893, has described and figured a species which appears to be *Dendrodoa glandaria*, or a closely related form, but which he identifies as *Styela aggregata* J. Rathke, and he refers to Traustedt as holding the same view. I find, however, on looking up the author's references to Traustedt that the latter does not mention *Dendrodoa*, but he does say of *Styela aggregata* that the "genitalorgane sind wie gewöhnlich beiderseits entwickelt" (Traustedt, 1893).

Kiær does not believe that the single branched ovary as it exists in *Dendrodoa* is a character of sufficient importance and constancy to justify the founding of a new genus upon it. Since, however, we now have three species in which the character is well defined and constant, they certainly do make a distinct group, so why not call the group a genus?

not conspicuously corrugated. Color very light brown, uniform throughout. (Figs. 6 and 7.)

Test.—Coriaceous, not hard, scarcely half a millimeter thick in thickest portions.

Mantle.—Not greatly developed; somewhat thicker than the test; composed mostly of longitudinal muscle fibers; does not readily separate from the test.

Branchial apparatus.—No siphons; orifices obscurely 4 lobed, rather close together, both situated at anterior end. Branchial tentacles simple, variable both in number, size, and distribution. In one specimen about 20 present—a group of 4 long, large ones near the dorsal tubercle; another group of about 10 large ones on the endostyle side, and the other 6 smaller ones situated 3 on each side, comparatively remote from one another. This arrangement of the tentacles apparently typical for the species, though less perfectly carried out in some specimens than in others. In some specimens not above 14 tentacles present. The peripharyngeal band close to the circle of branchial tentacles. Atrial tentacles present; unusually large; numerous.

Dorsal tubercle conspicuous, biscuit shaped, the hypophysis mouth horseshoe shaped, with out-turned limbs.

Branchial sac with 4 longitudinal folds on the right side and 3 on the left; 1 or 2 internal longitudinal vessels between each two folds. The number of vessels on the folds is as follows: Right side, first fold, 10 vessels; second, 4; third, 8; fourth, 4; left side, first fold, 11; second, 8; third, 4. (The folds are numbered from dorsal to ventral.) These numbers are quite constant.

Distance between transverse vessels varies from 0.19 mm. to 0.50 mm. The vessels are variable in size, but intermediate vessels—i. e., vessels crossing the stigmata—are rarely present. Dorsal lamina a plain narrow membrane, situated somewhat to the left of the median dorsal line.

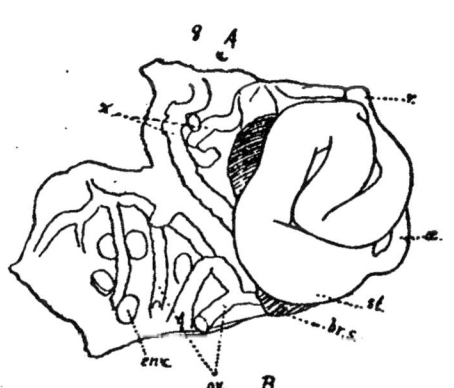

"Endocarps" present, prominent, and irregular in form, with a tendency to become lobed.

Digestive tract.—Situated on left side of branchial sac, closely coiled, the posterior half of the intestine running parallel, and in contact with, the œsophagus and anterior part of stomach. Œsophagus not as long as stomach. It issues from near the middle of the dorsal side of branchial sac, the dorsal lamina extending behind the opening and passing to its left. Stomach considerably longer than broad, somewhat broadest at œsophegeal end, not distinctly constricted off either from the œsophagus or from the intestine; smooth walled on its external surface, but inner surface thrown into numerous deep folds, causing it to resemble the psalterium of the ruminant stomach. (Fig. 8.)

Sexual organs.—Situated on right side of body only; ovary consisting of a basal portion, extending antero-posteriorly along the ventral side of the animal, and 4 branches from this basal part projecting forward and dorsalward. Testis situated around and among the branches of the ovary at their dorsal ends. Ova discharged into the atrial chamber, where they collect in its posterior portion to undergo development (fig. 8, *ov*.) (In this figure the visceral mass, lying loosely on the test, has been turned halfway around; so that the rectum, *r*, is made to point toward the *posterior* instead of toward the *anterior* end of the test. This makes the ovary seem on the *left* instead of on the *right* of the body.) Ova and sperm ripe in the same individual at the same time. Ova very large, 0.57 mm. in diameter; contains much food yolk.

This species is so distinct from either of the other two species of the genus, a comparison between which was made in connection with the description of *D. tuberculata*, that it would be superfluous to dwell upon the point. It is represented in the collection by a larger number of specimens than any of the other species, there being some hundreds present. All appear to come from St. Paul.

Styela greeleyi, new species.

General characteristics.—Body elongated, somewhat flattened; tapering slightly toward both ends, at the posterior abruptly contracted into a slender peduncle, which is from one and a half to two times as long as the body. Dimension of one of the largest specimens: Length of body, 1.8 cm.; greatest diameter, 1.1 cm.; length of peduncle, 4.3 cm. Color, yellowish brown, tinged with red on the anterior half. Siphons, bright orange red. Surface covered with longitudinal folds, which are less pronounced on the peduncle. Transverse folds present on the anterior half, but these possibly due to contraction. (Figs. 9 and 10.)

Test.—Tough, coriaceous, but scarcely 1 mm. thick even through the folds. Dull grayish white on the inner and cut surfaces.

Mantle.—Closely attached to test; musculature weak.

Branchial apparatus.—Siphons projecting slightly, both placed at anterior end close together, the atrial pointing straight forward, while the branchial is bent over so that the opening is directed ventrally. Branchial tentacles simple, of two sizes arranged in two concentric circles, the outer circle containing about 15 large and the inner about 30 small ones. Circles close to the peripharyngeal band. (Fig. 13.) Atrial tentacles filiform, numerous. Dorsal tubercle inconspicuous, the mouth of the hypophysis irregularly horseshoe shaped, close to the tentacles, which nearly hide

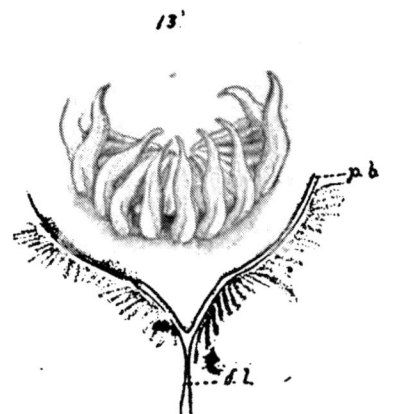

it. (Fig. 13.) Branchial sac with four folds on each side, the development of these folds varying with the size (age?) of the specimen. In smaller (younger?) specimens the folds on the left side more strongly developed than those on the right. In specimens 3.1 to 6.7 cm. (including peduncle), pair of folds next the endostyle had about 12 bars and those next dorsal lamina about 20. In specimen 0.85 to 1.8 cm. folds next endostyle had about 6 and those next dorsal lamina about 12 bars. Folds closely placed, only 3 to 5 bars between them. Transverse vessels of three sizes, a wide one (Tr_1, fig. 11) occurring at irregular intervals, and two narrower ones (Tr_2 and Tr_3), which usually alternate with each other. Intermediate transverse vessels (Tr_4) sometimes present, often dividing the series of stigmata into two. Meshes nearly square or longitudinally elongated with 4 to 6 (usually 5) long narrow stigmata. (Fig. 11.)

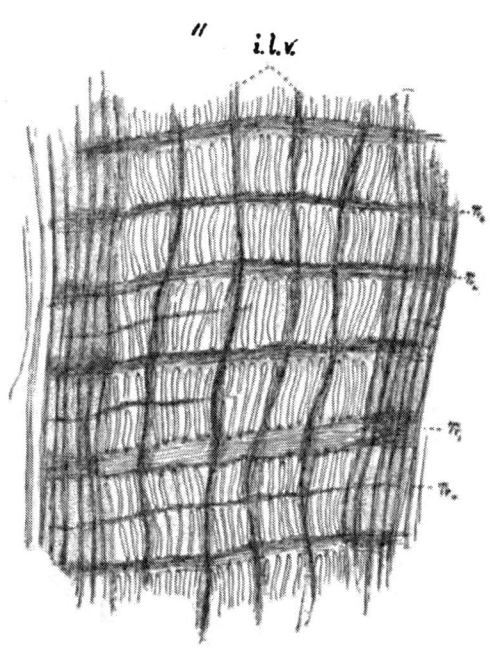

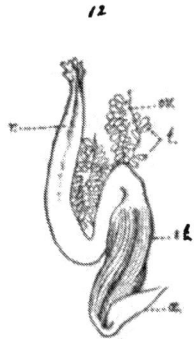

Dorsal lamina ribbed on one side by the vessels passing round the œsophagus.

Digestive tract.—Situated on the left side of branchial sac and making a narrow turn. Œsophagus short, opening from the dorsal side of the branchial sac near its posterior end. Stomach long and narrow, with numerous internal folds which show on the surface as longitudinal markings. Anal opening bilobed, each half cut into about six lobes. (Fig. 12.)

Sexual organs.—Gonads on each side of the body. Ovaries long, sausage shaped, ending in a short oviduct, those on the right side longer than those on the left. One of those on the left side placed in the loop of the intestine, the other beginning higher up and extending down under the stomach. Testis small, clustered in bunches over the ovaries. Endocarps rather numerous on the mantle.

The genus *Styela* is naturally divided into two sections—those in which the species are pedunculated, and those in which they are not. The species here described, of course, belongs to the first section. In this section *S. greeleyi* finds its nearest allies in *S. montereyensis* of the coast of California, and *S. clava*, Herdman, of the North Pacific. But it is quite distinct from either of these. So far as can be judged from the specimens at hand, it is a much smaller species than either of them. In general form it differs from *S. montereyensis* in its considerably more abrupt transition from body to peduncle; while from *S. clava* it differs distinctly by its lack of the prominent irregular tubercles of the test of the latter species. The collection contains 17 specimens of the species, all from St. Paul. Of these all but three or four are very small.

Boltenia elegans Herdman.

The three specimens in the collection, all from St. Paul Island, which I identify as this species, differ so trivially (our individuals are slightly darker in color and a little rougher on the surface) from specimens of the species taken by the *Albatross* (latitude 57° north, longitude 159° west, in 33 fathoms), that the correctness of the identification can not be doubted.

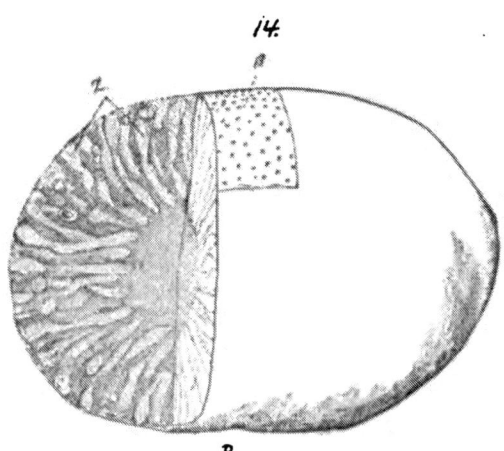

Polyclinum globosum, new species.

General character of the colony.—Massive, inclined toward the spherical form, attached by a small area only; apparently easily detached, since all the specimens at hand are freed from their original substrata. (Fig. 14.)

Dimensions of largest colony: Length, 45 mm.; least transverse diameter, 35 mm. The other colonies considerably smaller.

Color, greenish brown.

Zooids.—Large and numerous, though scarcely visible on the surface of the preserved colonies. The irregular systems contain numerous zooids, many of which are quite distant from the broad but inconspicuous atrial orifice common to the system. Positions approximately perpendicular to the surface of the colony. (Fig. 14 Z.)

Body distinctly separated into three regions, viz, thorax, abdomen, and postabdomen. (Fig. 15.)

Measurements of the zooids: Total length, 10 mm.; length of thorax, 4 mm.; length of postabdomen and abdomen, 6 mm.

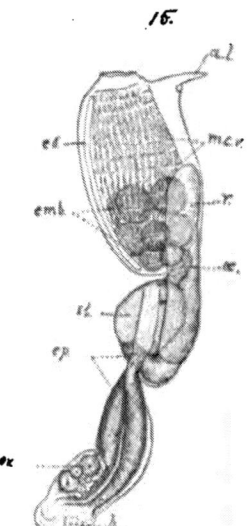

Test.—Small in quantity among the zooids, so close are these to one another; but a considerable mass in the middle of the colony in which no zooids occur. (Fig. 14.) Surface layer considerably denser and darker in color than the deeper portions, a few scattered sand grains embedded on the surface. The inner mass containing no zooids, rather firm in character; opaque white, contains many small cells, but no bladder cells; penetrated by the stolonic vessels of the zooids, though these are not numerous. A few scattered stellate crystals present.

Mantle.—Very thin, containing a few muscle fibers, mostly running lengthwise of the body; some circular fibers at the anterior end of the thorax encircling the siphons.

Branchial apparatus.—Branchial orifices indistinctly seen on the surface of the colony. (Fig. 14, area B, exaggerates the distinctness of the branchial orifices.) The common cloacal appertures wholly obliterated to superficial inspection. Branchial siphon found, after isolation of zooids, to be six lobed. Atrial siphon with a broad languet the distal edge of which is armed with three small processes (fig. 16). Branchial tentacles about 24 in number, rather large, though a few small; not forming a well-defined single circle. Rather close to the branchial orifice. Branchial sac well developed. About 15 series of stigmata and about 16 stigmata in each half series; these very regular in form and size. The interserial vessels broad and each containing a well-developed muscle band. (Fig. 15, *m. c. v.*)

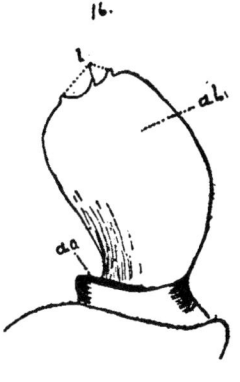

Dorsal languets long and slender, about one for each series of stigmata.

Digestive tract.—Œsophagus (fig. 15 *œ*) issuing posteriodorsally from the branchial sac, longer than the stomach; deflected to the right side by the rectum. Stomach spherical, smooth walled both without and within. Duodenal portion of the intestine with two well-marked constrictions. Rectal portion large and straight, runs far forward, nearly in the median dorsal line, which it reaches by a left curvature of the duodenal portion. (Fig. 15.)

Sexual organs.—Gonads contained in the large pear-shaped pedunculated postabdomen; ovary a well-defined mass, confined to the enlarged posterior portion of the postabdomen. (Fig. 15, *ov.*)

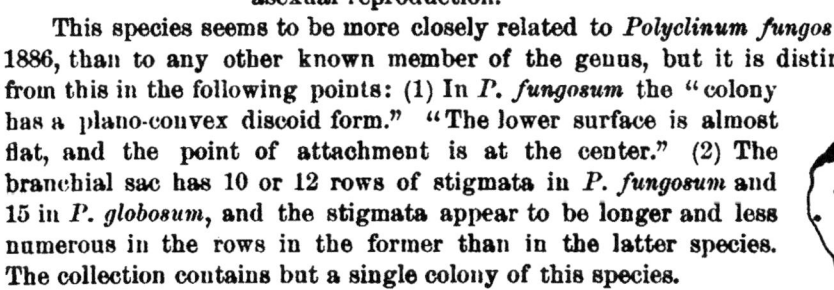

The ova pass into the atrial chamber, where they take a position in its posterior portion and to the right side. The larvae are developed in this incubatory chamber. No male gonads have been found in any of the specimens examined. No buds have been seen; and as the colonies at hand are all in a state of prolific sexual reproduction, it seems probable that in this species there is an alternation of periods of sexual and asexual reproduction.

This species seems to be more closely related to *Polyclinum fungosum* Herdman, 1886, than to any other known member of the genus, but it is distinctly different from this in the following points: (1) In *P. fungosum* the "colony has a plano-convex discoid form." "The lower surface is almost flat, and the point of attachment is at the center." (2) The branchial sac has 10 or 12 rows of stigmata in *P. fungosum* and 15 in *P. globosum*, and the stigmata appear to be longer and less numerous in the rows in the former than in the latter species. The collection contains but a single colony of this species.

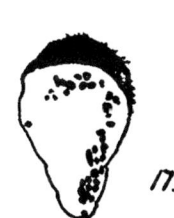

Polyclinum pannosum, new species.

General character of colony.—Form variable, from quite regularly pear-shaped to depressed and irregularly elliptical. Not distinctly pedunculated, though some colonies show a tendency in this direction. Largest colony in collection measures 3 cm.

to 2 cm. to 1½ cm. Unyielding to the touch, dirty greenish-brown in color. Portions of the surface of the colonies smooth, almost shiny, but for the most part a surface crust of test becomes broken up and the broken fragments partially or wholly peeled off. Where these pieces are fully removed sand adheres to the underlying exposed test. By reason of the conditions of the surface test thus described the colonies usually present a ragged appearance, hence the specific name chosen. (Fig. 17 A y.)

Test.—Matrix firm, relatively large in quantity, there being a large central core in each colony, into which the zooids do not reach, and the zooids themselves are rather remote, making the intervening test considerable in quantity. Cells numerous, of many sizes, some of them large. The cells contain a diffuse greenish coloring matter, to which is due the tint of the test when seen in section. The central core of test penetrated by a wide areolar mesh work of rather fine fibers. (Fig. 17 A.)

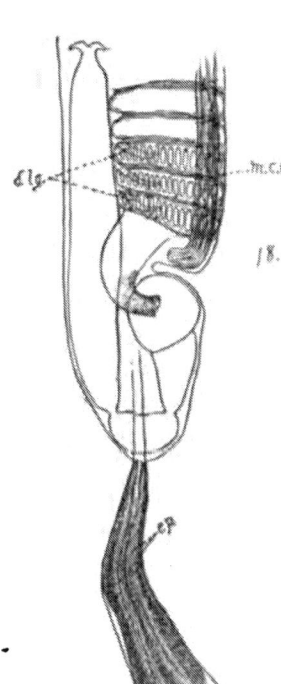

Zooids.—Moderately numerous, not visible on surface view of the colony. Owing to their variously twisted condition and the differing angles which they form with the surface of the colony, the entire length of a single zooid is seldom seen uncut on radial sections of the whole colony. Average length of individuals, about 6 mm., about one-half of which is postabdomen. Thorax about 2 mm.; abdomen about 1 mm. Postabdomen joined to the postero-ventral side of the abdomen, somewhat to the left side, by a narrow peduncle. (Fig. 18.)

Mantle.—Feebly developed. Longitudinal muscle fibers in distinct bands; circular fibers almost wholly absent, except in the siphons, and here they are not strongly developed.

Branchial apparatus.—Orifices very indistinctly seen on the surface of the colony. On removal from test, branchial siphon found to be encircled by six unequal rather pointed lobes. Atrial languet not easily seen intact, of moderate length, broad at base, tapering rapidly to a blunt point, which, however, sometimes shows traces of two or three lobes.

Branchial sac removed whole from test with much difficulty, this due to the delicacy of it and the mantle, and the fact of its being thrust up more or less sidewise into the specially dense, firm, and rather thick layer of surface test. This displacement apparently caused by the numerous large embryos contained in the atrial chamber.

Organs of the peripharyngeal region distinguished with much difficulty; ganglion moderately large, tentacles about 25 in number, of different sizes, the largest ones but few, not large. All situated close around the base of the siphon. Branchial sac containing about 12 series (in some specimens 13, and some apparently 10 or 11) of stigmata. Cilia of the stigmata unusually long and stout. In some specimens the stigmata quite pointed and with a peculiar process, sometimes of considerable length at the ends. A well-developed muscle band in each interserial space. Dorsal languets long, sometimes reaching more than halfway across the sac, about equal in number to the series of stigmata. (Fig. 18, *dlg.*)

Digestive tract.—Œsophagus rather wide at its mouth, issuing from nearly the middle of the posterior end of the branchial sac, distinctly curved so as to enter the stomach on its right dorsal side. Stomach globular, smooth walled. Intestinal loop rather wide, slightly shorter than the combined length of œsophagus and stomach. Two well-marked constrictions in the intestine at the base of the loop, these including between them the base of the U-shaped loop; the rectum passing to the left of the œsophagus to reach the atrial chamber. Anus sometimes with a wide, flaring lip. (Fig. 18.)

Sexual organs.—Ovary not large, situated far back in the post-abdomen, behind the testis. The entire post-abdomen so filled with mesenchymatous cells that the sexual organs are much obscured; no distinct lobulation of either ovary or testes observable. The embryos, developing in the atrial chamber, greatly distend and distort this cavity.

This species appears to be more closely related to *P. aurantium*, Milne-Edwards, than to any other member of the genus. The last-named species is, however, described by both Milne-Edwards, 1842, and Lahille, 1890, as having a gelatinous test, and no mention is made by either of these authors of the network of fibers in the test. This latter character, I take it, constitutes a distinct difference between the two. The presence of such a network seems to be of such rare occurrence in *Polyclinum* that were it present in *P. aurantium*, Lahille, whose studies were largely morphological, would have noted it. Furthermore, according to the figure of a zooid of *P. aurantium*, given by Milne-Edwards (Pl. III, fig. 4, *b*), the postabdomen of this species is relatively much longer than in *P. pannosum*.

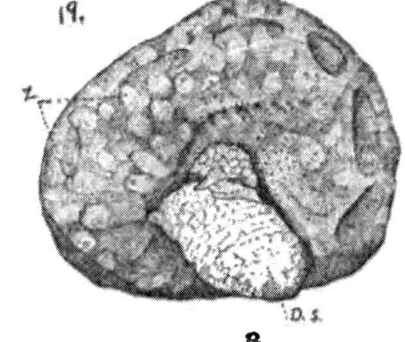

There are about two dozen colonies of this species in the collection, all from St. Paul Island.

Aplidiopsis jordani, new species.

General character of the colony.—Massive, irregularly polyhedral in form, the three dimensions not greatly different. Attached by a small area only (fig. 19). Quite hard and unyielding to the touch; surface rather uneven. Light gray in color, with the yellowish zooids distinctly visible. A thin surface layer of test considerably harder and less transparent than the interior portions, which latter is quite transparent. A few sand grains imbedded on the surface.

Greatest diameter of the one colony in the collection, 2.3 cm.; least diameter, 1.5 mm.

Cells in test very numerous, rather uniform in size. No vessels present in the test.

Zooids.—Rather large and numerous, readily seen on the surface of the colony. No systems present, each zooid opening to the surface by its own atrial orifice. Many of the individuals placed at very oblique but differing angles to the surface of the colony, so that they are crossed by and wound around one another. Post-abdomen not pedunculated. A finger-like ectodermal process projecting from posterior end of body. Total length about 8 mm., one-fourth of which is branchial sac, another fourth intestinal loop, and the other half post-abdomen. (The post-abdomen outlined in fig. 20 is unusually short.) Post-abdomen very large at its posterior end, and is dense and opaque with the contained generative and mesenchyme cells. It gradually narrows toward its attachment to the abdomen, but is not pedunculated, it being at the junction fully as thick as the abdomen itself.

Mantle.—Very thin, though its ectodermal layer presents, particularly in posterior part of the post-abdomen, a layer of well-defined epitheloid cells. Musculature consisting of a few small, widely separated bundles of longitudinal fibers and a still smaller number of circular fibers, the latter confined to the anterior region of the animal. Owing to this disposition of the circular fibers, in the contracted state the anterior end of the thorax becomes much smaller and denser than the posterior end. But few mesenchyme cells in the mantle.

Branchial apparatus.—Branchial orifices readily seen on the surface of the colony by the aid of a hand lens, but the atrial orifices scarcely visible; former circular in outline, no lobes distinguishable till the zooids are removed from the test, when the branchial siphon is found to be obscurely six lobed, while the atrial siphon, often considerably elongated, has no constant lobulation. In some zooids a large lobe, undoubtedly representing the atrial languet of some species, is seen on the dorsal side of the atrial orifice (fig. 20). Owing to the persistently contracted condition of the anterior portion of the branchial sac the number and arrangement of the branchial tentacles have not been determined; it is, however, found that they are rather small and few in number. Peripharyngeal band situated close to the branchial siphon. Ganglion not large, spherical, distinctly seen through the mantle in uncontracted zooids. Hypophyseal duct distinct, wide mouthed, well ciliated. Endostyle of moderate size, never greatly tortuous, extends forward nearly to the base of the branchial siphon. Branchial sac well developed, 12 or 13 series of stigmata, each half series containing about 15 stigmata. Well developed interserial muscle bundles. Dorsal languets at least as numerous as the series of stigmata; highly developed, sickle shaped, with the concave side directed forward, the epitheloid cells of the wall of this side considerably higher than those of the convex or posterior side.

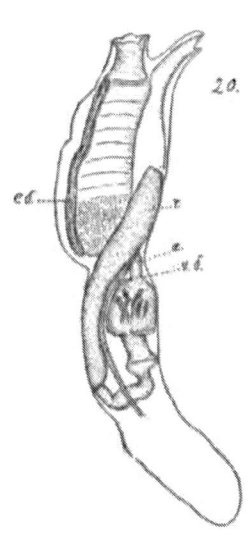

Digestive tract.—Œsophagus about equaling the stomach in length, stomach somewhat longer than broad when not contracted, extension of loop behind stomach about equal to the combined length of the œsophagus and stomach; rectal portion of intestine passing to left of the œsophagus to reach the mid dorsal line in the region of the branchial sac. Stomach wall with a few irregular longitudinal thickenings, but no well-defined folds.

Sexual organs.—Gonads contained in the large post-abdomen, the testis consisting of a large number of closely crowded lobes, occupying its posterior two-thirds, while the ovary is confined to its narrower anterior third. The ovary is situated close behind the intestinal loop. Vas deferens, well filled with ripe sperm, passes forward, sometimes on the right and sometimes on the left of the loop of the intestine. No embryos or ripe ova in the specimens at hand. No buds seen.

This species, which I take pleasure in dedicating to President Jordan, belongs to a group of Ascidians, the exact systematic position of which has troubled me for some years. It has several representatives on the coast of California, so I have had ample opportunity for studying it; notwithstanding this, I have not been able to fully satisfy myself as to whether a new genus should be established for it or not. That it belongs to the family Polyclinidae there can be no doubt. The possession by the zooids of a large, well-marked post-abdomen in which are situated the reproductive organs and heart leaves no room for question on this point. When, however, the effort is made to determine with which of the known genera of this family the group is most closely allied, much difficulty is experienced.

The entire absence of systems or coenobia in the colonies leads us, in the first place, to compare it with those Polyclinidae presenting a like deviation from the prevailing condition in this particular.

In the genus *Tylobranchion*, Herdman, no common cloacal apertures are present, according to the author, but this is about the only resemblance between the two groups; the most distinctive difference being, perhaps, the possession of papillae on the internal transverse vessels of the branchial sac in *Tylobranchion*. *Sigillina*, Savigny, is another genus in which the common cloaca is wanting; but the shortness of the branchial sac and great length and slenderness of the post-abdomen are characters which preclude the admission of our species to this group. *Sigillina australis*, Savigny, the only species known of this genus, has but four series of stigmata, while there are never less than six or seven present in any of the representatives of the group now under consideration, and the rule is that twelve or thirteen series are present.

As regards the post-abdomen in *Sigillina*, its great length, relative to the length of the rest of the animal, and its tenuity, set it off very sharply not only from our forms, but also from all other known species of the family.

The genus *Atopogaster*, Herdman, contains one species, at least, viz., *A. aurantiaca*, in which, according to this author, there are no systems or common cloacal apertures, and there are certainly some rather weighty considerations in favor of regarding this group as the one to which the present species is most closely related. Several points, however, the most important being the transverse folds of the stomach wall in *Atopogaster*, stand rather seriously in the way of doing this. There is considerable variability in the character of the stomach wall in our species, and the folds are never well pronounced. Such as are present, however, incline distinctly toward the lengthwise instead of toward the crosswise direction of the stomach.

I am disposed to place somewhat less reliance than some writers have done on this character as an index to relationships; nevertheless a condition so unusual as a transverse folding must, as our knowledge now stands, be regarded as of real systematic value.

I have resolved, after much deliberation, to place the species, for the present at least, in the genus *Aplidiopsis*, Lahille. There are certainly some objections to this, the most considerable being found again in the structure of the stomach wall. Lahille instituted this genus for the reception of those Polyclinidae in the restricted sense in which he recognizes this family, which have a smooth walled stomach, no torsion of the intestinal loop, and a nonpedunculated post abdomen. The smooth wall of the stomach, therefore, is one of the important characters on which the genus rests, and the placing of my species in it does some violence to it, for there is certainly a strong tendency, to say the least, for the stomach wall here to become folded, i. e., there are more or less pronounced and regular thickened areas in the wall, and in connection with these, at least in many of the preserved specimens, there are indications of folding. (Fig. 20.) But in some specimens, again, I can detect scarcely a trace of either thickening or folding, and there are so many and close resemblances between our species and *A. sarsii*, Huitfeldt-Kaas, 1896, from the Norwegian coast, that I am fully convinced of the very close affinities of the two. I have consequently deemed it the wiser course to place it here rather than to add another to the already long list of rather illy-defined genera into which the Polyclinidae are divided. In this connection I can not refrain, after having spent much time in examining the stomachs of numerous species and genera, and in critically reading the utterances of other writers, from quoting that master zoologist, Milne-Edwards, 1842, on this point. After describing the stomach of his *Amaroucium argus* (transferred by Giard, 1872, largely on account of the structure of the stomach, to the genus *Morchellium*), he says: "Mais si l' on descendait à des caractères de cet ordre pour en faire la base des divisions génériques, on serait conduit à multiplier inutilement ces coupes et on rendrait les déterminations d' une difficulté extrême." The advance of knowledge since this remark was made has undoubtedly shown that the character of the stomach wall is of diagnostic importance, but that it in itself can be relied upon in all cases, even as a distinctive specific mark, to say nothing of its generic value, I do not believe. The species is represented in the collection by a single colony from St. Paul Island.

Amaroucium kincaidi, new species.

Colony cake-like, irregular in outline, but always depressed. When attached to cylindrical bodies of small diameter, as seaweeds, which seems to be the usual habit, colony entirely incircling these. Firm and unyielding to the touch. In color, little sand on the surface, zooids showing through the test quite distinctly. Common atrial orifices large and open.

Dimensions of largest colony, 54 mm. to 31 mm. to 21 mm.; of smallest colony, 27 mm. to 20 mm. to 17 mm.

Test.—Surface layer, which is quite thick, containing so much brownish-gray coloring matter that the transparency characteristic of the interior portions is here wholly obscured. Cells of the test vary; abundant fibers absent. Sand grains penetrating the entire mass, though not numerous, not incrusting the surface. Only a small interior portion of test into which the zooids do not reach.

Mantle.—Longitudinal muscle fibers in bands, though not as completely separated from one another as in many species. Circular fibers almost wholly absent excepting in the siphons, but not numerous even here.

Zooids.—Visible, though not distinctly so, on the surface of the colony. Arranged in definite, circular systems, each containing about six or eight individuals. Standing at various angles to the surface of the colony, and considerably contorted, so that they appear only in fragments on cut surfaces of the colony, whatever be the direction of the section. Subdivisions of the body not distinct. Size, medium; total length, about 8 mm.; thorax, about 2.5 mm.; abdomen, about 1.5 mm., and post-abdomen about 4 mm. Peduncular portion of post-abdomen easily noticeable, though not conspicuous as compared with many other species (fig. 21). An ectodermal appendage of the mantle at the posterior end of the post-abdomen.

Branchial apparatus.—Branchial orifice scarcely recognizable on the surface of the colony. Common atrial orifice, large and open, at least in some colonies.

branchial siphon, with six quite regular, broad, low lobes. Atrial siphon with a dorsal languet, but this apparently never of considerable length, usually broad and blunt, sometimes, probably usually, three lobed, sometimes two lobed, and at least in one instance observed, only one lobed. Contraction of branchial sac about equal throughout its length, in no portion so great as to render the structure indistinguishable. Ganglion moderate in size, spherical, visible through the body wall. Tentacles fairly well developed, about 24 in number, of unequal length, somewhat more removed from base of siphon than in the other species of the genus described in this paper. About 16 series of rather small, short, elliptical stigmata. A well-developed muscle band in each interserial space of the sac. Dorsal languets not conspicuous.

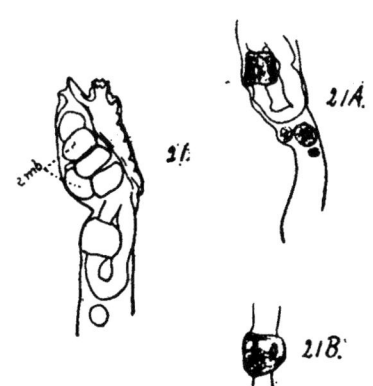

Digestive tract.—Unusually small and contracted. Œsophagus very short in proportion to its diameter, at least as presented in all the specimens examined. Stomach small and contracted, often apparently but little greater in diameter than the rectal portion of the intestine. Wall never with distinct longitudinal folds, but never smooth. In some zooids it presents merely thickened patches of irregular shape and unequal size, while in others there are distinct indications of areolation. In some individuals the areolae are elongated lengthwise of the organ, while in others their greatest extent is crosswise of it, but this last condition may be the result of contraction. (Figs. 21 A and 21 B.)

Remaining portions of the tract without characteristic features. The constrictions of the intestine in the base of the loop irregular, but apparently never very pronounced.

Sexual organs.—Ovary immediately behind the intestinal loop in the peduncular portion of the post-abdomen. Ova large, containing much yolk; not numerous. Testis situated behind the ovary and extending to the extreme posterior end of the post-abdomen; composed of many small lobes; vas deferens not conspicuous.

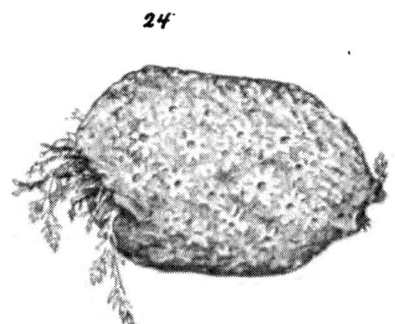

Embryos developed to the completed tadpole stage in the atrial chamber, this becoming much distended by them. (Fig. 21).

There are four colonies of this species in the collection, all from St. Paul Island.

Amaroucium pribilovense, new species.

General character of the colony.—Massive, regular in outline, smooth surface, subglobular, very little or no indication of pedunculation, though usually attached by small area only. Greatest diameter of largest colony 5.5 cm., least diameter 3 cm. (Fig. 24.)

Unyielding to the touch; dark gray with a slight olive tinge; considerable sand adhering to and embedded in the surface. Zooids quite distinctly visible on the surface. Testicular mass not large in quantity, the zooids being rather crowded, particularly in the larger colonies. A surface layer considerably denser and darker colored than the deeper portions. Sand grains scattered over the surface and also penetrating the whole test mass. Cells numerous in the test, but no vessels.

Zooids.—Closely crowded, particularly in the larger colonies, quite distinctly visible on the surface of the colony, each standing generally at nearly a right angle to the surface. Systems usually distinct, number of zooids in each usually small—6, 8, or 10, sometimes more. The three divisions of the body distinct, but not constricted off from one another. Length of thorax 3 mm., length of abdomen 3 mm., of post-abdomen 5 to 10 mm., depending on the extent of development of the testis.

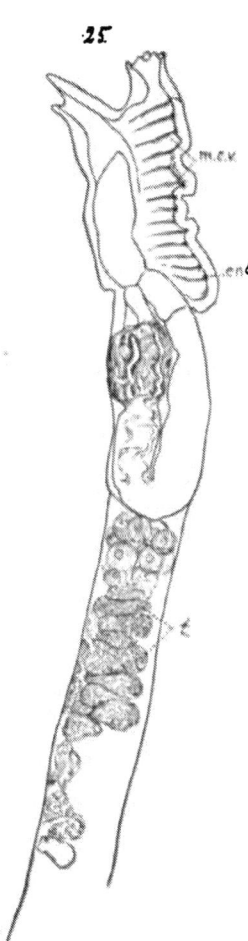

Post-abdomen when fully developed somewhat, though not greatly, larger at its posterior than at its anterior end. (Fig. 25.)

Mantle.—Feebly developed. Circular muscle fibers almost wholly absent, they being restricted to a few scattering ones around the branchial siphon. Longitudinal fibers grouped in distinct bundles, though these not numerous.

Branchial apparatus.—Branchial orifices easily recognizable on the surface of the colony by the aid of hand lens, though no lobes visible. Common atrial orifices moderately large. When removed from the test, branchial siphon found to possess six quite distinct and regular lobes. Atrial siphon with a broad dorsal languet, usually two-lobed, but sometimes three-lobed. This languet very variable in length, in some zooids the siphon departing but slightly from the normal six-lobed condition.

Anterior half of the branchial sac usually considerably more contracted than the posterior half. The globular ganglion seen without difficulty when the anterior end is examined after having been cut off. Tentacles apparently about twenty in number, of different lengths, about half of them being long and stout. The circle situated close to the siphon.

Branchial sac well developed. Fifteen series of stigmata certainly present in some individuals, but apparently twelve or thirteen in others—possibly immature ones. Interserial muscle bands present; posterior end of the endostyle invariably produced into a U-shaped loop in the preserved specimens.

Digestive tract.—Œsophagus issuing from the postero-dorsal angle of the branchial sac; form and proportions of the tract as a whole conforming closely to the usual type for the genus. Stomach somewhat barrel-shaped, folded longitudinally, but the folds are irregular and are neither conspicuous nor numerous, the number being about seven. In addition to the folds, or rather furrows, which never involve the entire surface, there is a tendency for the surface between the furrows to become areolated in many specimens. (Fig. 25.)

Sexual organs.—Ovary immediately behind and in contact with the intestinal loop, small in volume as compared with the testis, which latter is very large, it appearing to constitute almost the whole of the long post-abdomen.

Vas deferens filled with sperm in the specimens at hand, consequently large and conspicuous; passes to the left of the intestinal loop. No embryos seen.

The simplicity of the systems of zooids, the two-lobed atrial languet, and the few remote furrows in the wall of the stomach are the most distinctive characters of this species. In the first-mentioned particular it agrees more nearly with *A. nordmani*, Milne-Edwards, than with any other species of the genus.

So far as I have been able to ascertain, this is the only instance in the genus in which the atrial languet is two lobed, it being in all other species either one or three lobed.

A collection contains a half dozen colonies, all from St. Paul Island.

Amarouoium snodgrassi, new species.

General character of the colony.—Form quite variable, but always depressed and cake-like. Area of attachment considerably smaller than the superior free surface. Greatest transverse diameter of largest colony 7 cm.; greatest width 5 cm., greatest thickness 2.8 cm. Rather soft and yielding to the touch. Light gray in color, excepting where covered with sand, which is quite abundant on some of the colonies. The zooids, indistinctly seen on the top surface of the colonies, but distinctly visible on the edges, where the outermost ones show throughout their entire length, as they reach entirely through the thickness of the colony. (Fig. 22.)

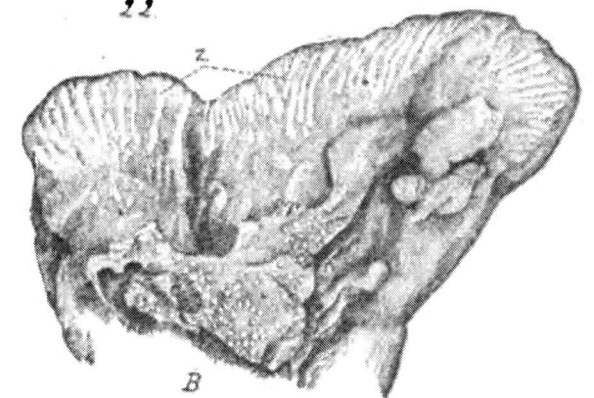

Test.—Not in great quantity, there being no central core into which the zooids do not enter. A few sand grains scattered through entire mass. Cells very numerous, but no vessels or fibers present.

Zooids.—Large, each reaching entirely through the thickness of the colony; quite straight, and placed nearly at a right angle to the surface of the colony. As seen on a cut surface of a vertical section of the colony, the thoracic-abdominal portion distinctly set off from the post-abdominal portion by the greater thickness of the former and the lighter but more opaque color of the latter. Post-abdomen joined to the abdomen by a very long, slender peduncle. Total length of zooid from 2 cm. to 2.5 cm.; of this about 4 or 5 mm. are thorax, about an equal part abdomen, and the remainder—12 or 15 mm.—post-abdomen. Systems not readily seen either on surface of colony or on horizontal sections of same; dissection discovers them to be present, however, with about 8 or 10 zooids in each.

Mantle.—Musculature not highly developed. Longitudinal fibers, as usual, in bands; circular fibers present, but confined to anterior half of thorax.

Branchial apparatus.—Branchial orifices found with difficulty on surface of colony; common atrial openings quite large, though collapsed and not obvious until searched after. Branchial siphon with six wide, well-defined, though not prominent, lobes. Atrial languet three lobed, at least usually, broad and never very long. Anterior end of thorax usually considerably contracted, so that the various contained organs are

seen with difficulty. Ganglion not spherical, not large. Tentacles not numerous, apparently about twelve, presenting a peculiar distorted, shriveled appearance, situated very close around the base of the siphon. (Fig. 23 A).

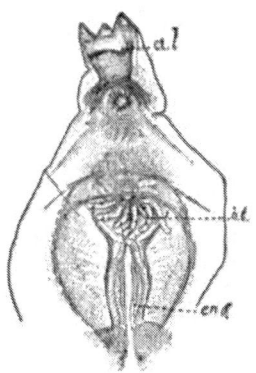

Branchial sac consisting of about twelve series of long, narrow, regular stigmata. A well-developed muscle band in each interserial space. (Fig. 23 B.) Dorsal languets long and slender, one for each series of stigmata. Endostyle nearly straight, moderate in size.

Digestive tract.—Œsophagus issuing from the branchial sac at its postero-dorsal angle. Nothing characteristic in the general form and proportions of the tract as a whole. Stomach distinctly longer than broad. Folds of its wall distinct, about six extending the entire length of the organ, and in addition two or three shorter and narrower ones on one side; in some cases these strongly suggesting the areolated condition (fig. 23). Rectum terminating in a broad, trumpet-shaped anus.

Sexual organs.—Ovary small, situated in the post-abdomen, a short distance behind but not in contact with the intestinal loop. Testis occupying nearly the whole of the remainder of the long post-abdomen. The numerous rather small regular lobes are distinctly visible, those of the anterior narrower portion of the post-abdomen forming a single row only in many specimens. Vas deferens conspicuous, passing to left of intestinal loop. No embryos seen.

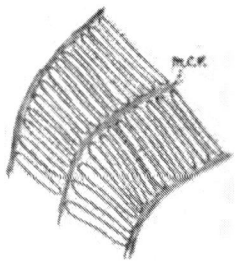

This species has much in common with *A. pribilovense* when the two are compared with reference to the zooids only; though from this standpoint they are rendered specifically quite distinct by differences in size, in the atrial languets, and in the folds of the stomach wall. The greatest difference between them, however, as will be noticed, is in the general character of the colony. These species would appear to be somewhat closely related to *A. mutabile*, Sars, though, as I know this form only by the figures and partial description given by Huitfeldt-Kaas, 1896, I am unable to make a complete comparison between them. *A. mutabile* is, however, represented as having a much more distinctly 3-lobed atrial languet than either of my species, and also with only 4 furrows or folds in the stomach. It is therefore well set off from the present species. There are about 8 colonies of this species in the collection, all from St. George Island.

Amaroucium dubium, new species.

I designate by this name a species of Amaroucium collected by Mr. Leonhard Stejneger at Copper Island during his visit there in the summer of 1897. There are only three fragments of colonies at hand, and as these are considerably eroded, apparently from having been torn from their anchorage and washed about by the waves, and as the zooids are all in a state of extreme contraction, I have hesitated very much about describing it as a new species. As, however, sufficient information concerning its structure is obtainable to show it to be different from any hitherto described species of the genus, I have concluded that a description of it would be justifiable, even though this must be more or less incomplete.

General character of the colony.—Apparently flat and incrusting. Specimens at hand closely adherent to and somewhat interwoven with laminaria roots. Quite dense to the touch; a considerable quantity of sand imbedded in portions of the test; this rather more abundant in the deeper parts than on the surface. Greatest dimension of largest piece 3 cm., average thickness about 1 cm. Color grayish white; in portions where sand is absent somewhat opalescent, so that the zooids can be seen through the test with some distinctness.

Zooids; general characters.—Probably arranged in systems, each containing but comparatively few individuals; but the specimens at hand do not permit of certainty on this point. Moderately numerous, rather irregularly distributed, there being considerable areas of test which contain none at all. Placed at various angles to the surface of the colony. Removed from the test with much difficulty. All in condition of extreme contraction. Owing to this fact and the well-nigh impossibility of removing them complete from the test, the length of the individuals can not be determined with any accuracy, but this not more than a few millimeters—4 or 5. Thickness considerable as compared with length, even after contraction is taken into consideration. Regions of the body very indistinct. Post-abdomen apparently about as long as combined thorax and abdomen; broad at its origin, and tapering rapidly back to its termination.

Branchial apparatus.—Little information obtainable concerning the orifices. Branchial siphon short, its 5 lobes well marked, probably in living specimens quite long. Atrial siphon inconspicuous, with a wide, short languet, apparently having but one lobe. Thorax very dense, owing in considerable degree to the large quantity of mesenchymatous tissue and the thickness of the epithelial layer of the mantle; for in spite of the extreme state of contraction the musculature is not developed to an unusual extent.

As nearly as can be determined the branchial sac contains about 10 series of stigmata.

Digestive tract.—Intestinal loop very short, indistinguishable in its several parts excepting the stomach and rectum, the latter being very wide and filled with dark brown faecal matter not formed into pellets. Stomach somewhat broader than long. Walls longitudinally ridged on the inner surface, though the ridges are not always regular and parallel. Apparently about 10 or 12 in number.

Reproductive organs.—Ovary forming a compact mass situated some distance behind the intestinal loop. Not large, so thoroughly embedded in the mesenchymatous tissue(?)—food yolk—contained in the post-abdomen that it is found with difficulty. Testis not distinctly lobed, but large and massive, occupying most of the post-abdomen.

Embryos present in the atrial chamber of a few zooids.

It is possible that careful study of more material of this species will prove there are in reality two species represented here, distinguished by difference in size of zooids, form of post-abdomens, ridges in the wall of stomachs, and perhaps in some other particulars. But with the small number of specimens now available for examination it is impossible to differentiate two such species with any satisfaction.

Synoicum irregulare, new species.

General character of the colony.—In all cases distinctly lobed, but the lobes very variable in size and shape. In some instances they are separate almost to the base of the colony, while in others the upper half or even less of the entire length of the lobe is free from the common basal mass. Some of the lobes decidedly enlarged at the summit, others not so. An occasional lobe stands out at nearly a right angle to those with which it is in closest relation. Rarely any free spaces between the free portions of the lobes. No longitudinal furrows on the lobes marking the intervals between the zooids, though the zooids quite clearly visible through the test on the sides of the lobes. Surface of the test at the bases of the lobes and of the basal undivided mass often shows well-marked transverse corrugations (fig. 26). Color of the lobes milk white; of the basal portions grayish. This appears to be the predominating color characterization, but some colonies gray throughout. Very little sand or other foreign substance on the surface. Test relatively large in quantity, semicartilagenous, no distinct surface layer. Cells very numerous. Basal portions traversed by a few vessels. Height of largest colony, 3 cm.; length of longest lobe in this colony, 17 mm.; thickness of base of this lobe, 8 mm.; thickness of summit of same lobe, 13 mm. These values would not appear to be greatly above the average.

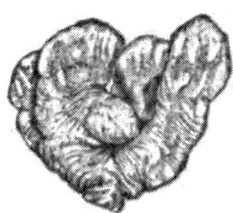

Zooids.—From two or three to eight or ten in each lobe. Not visible on the summit of the lobes in any of the specimens at hand, but quite distinctly so on the sides of the lobes in some colonies. Of large size, always at least as long as the lobes of the colony, usually extending to very near the base of the colony. Average length about 17 mm. Of this, considerably more than half is post-abdomen. Thorax relatively very short in all specimens at hand, but this largely due to great contraction. Post-abdomen not pedunculated (fig. 28). Condition as to systems in doubt. Apparently a common cloaca not usually present, but material at hand does not permit final determination of the point.

In some colonies zooids in a peculiar state of disorganization. (This subject more fully treated in another connection.)

Musculature consisting almost exclusively of longitudinal fibers; these not disposed in bundles to the usual extent in compound ascidians.

Branchial apparatus.—Neither of the orifices found with certainty on the surface of the colony in any of the specimens at hand. In the few colonies in which the thorax is present at all, so much contracted and so thick walled that its structure could be but imperfectly determined. Branchial siphon six-lobed; these thick and rather obscure. Atrial orifice obscurely unequally lobed. A short and thick atrial languet present; its lobulation not determined. Tentacles not large or numerous, of unequal sizes.

At least 17 series of stigmata, the individual stigmata exceedingly small and obscure, though the series fairly well marked by the heavy muscle band in each interstigmatic space. This muscle band as broad as, or broader than, the stigmatic area (fig. 28, *m. c. v*).

Endostyle broad, not greatly tortuous. No information concerning the dorsal languets.

Digestive apparatus.—Loop rather wide, not twisted, particularly characterized by the great thickness of the rectal limb.

Œsophagus exceptionally broad, particularly at its mouth; much narrower at its entrance into the stomach. Stomach apparently nearly spherical in its normal form, but usually broader than long in preserved specimens. Its entire wall covered with small, rather uniform, thickened patches or areolations (fig. 28). Length of the loop behind the stomach considerably greater than combined length of œsophagus and stomach. Rectal portion of intestine greatly enlarged in most specimens. It reaches the dorsal side of the branchial sac by turning at a short angle immediately behind the sac.

Reproductive organs.—Situated in the long, broad post-abdomen. Ovary in the form of a long, narrow band placed at one side of the post-abdomen (fig. 28, *ov.*), the ova distinctly amoeboid, and without recognizable follicular epithelium or "test" cells. No oviduct observed. Testis distinguished with difficulty (excepting when containing ripe sperm) from the great mass of mesenchymatous material by which the post-abdomen is filled. Vas deferens not seen. Embryos develop in packages in cavities of the test (fig. 27). No budding seen.

(See end of paper for account of sexual reproduction of this species.)

This species is certainly closely related to *S. turgens* Phipps, and at first I was much inclined to consider it to be identical with that species. There seem, however, to be several points of difference between them so considerable as to make it necessary to regard them as distinct species.

In the first place *S. turgens* as figured by both Savigny, 1816 (Pl. III, fig. 3), and Sars (see Bonnevie, 1896, p. 12, and Pl. IV, fig. 36), has the lobes in general much more separate than is the case in *S. irregulare*. And in his description Savigny speaks of the systems as being in the form of solid cylinders "isolated or associated by their peduncles." Again, our species shows no trace of the channels on the surface of the lobes marking the intervals between the zooids, such as are described and figured by Savigny in *S. turgens*. The systems and common cloacal orifices of *S. turgens* are, according to the authors already mentioned, very distinct, while in *S. irregulare*, as will be noted from my description, there is much doubt about their being present at all.

As concerns the zooids, it would appear that the two forms agree very closely, though it is hardly possible that the branchial sac of *S. turgens* could be so closely contracted, and the stigmata thereby so greatly obscured, as is the case in all the material of *S. irregulare* at my disposal, without having been mentioned by Savigny.

From *S. incrustatum*, Sars, Huitfeldt-Kaas, 1896, the only other species of the genus, the present species differs so markedly that a detailed contrast between them would be superfluous.

The collection contains about a dozen colonies and pieces of colonies of this most interesting ascidian, all, so far as my information goes, from St. Paul Island.

Both *Synoicum irregulare* and *Polyclinum pannosum* present interesting conditions in connection with their sexual reproduction. I describe that shown by the first-named species only. Unfortunately, however, the collection does not contain sufficient specimens to enable me to make the account as full as might be desired.

In the formal description of the species I have pointed out that the thorax is very small relatively, and is much contracted and so dense and opaque as to make it impossible to distinguish the branchial sac with any clearness. This is the condition in all the colonies at hand in which the thorax of the zooids is found at all. But in most of the colonies a great proportion of the zooids are wholly without the thorax. It frequently happens that, although the lobes of the colonies are of nearly normal size, the upper half or more of some of them may contain no zooids or parts of zooids, and the test may be entirely solid, i. e., without cavities such as are usually found in preserved specimens of compound ascidians in which the zooids have withdrawn upon killing into the deeper portions of the test. This condition is the result of degeneration of the zooids, or at least their anterior portions. Post-abdomens alone are found in great numbers in such colonies. Frequently these do not differ in any respect, either in form, size, or composition, from others that are still connected with branchial sacs. I have not been able to follow the process of disappearance, either of the thorax or of the solidification of the test in the parts of the lobes containing no zooids. It is very possible that the condition of the thorax as I have described it is not typical for the species, but is a result of the retrogressive process having already set in. Of this, however, I have no certain proof. Examination of the free post-abdomens shows them to be densely filled with a material that is for the most part undoubtedly of the nature of food yolk. This does not differ in any essential particular from the food material that is found in many compound ascidians. When fully elaborated it consists of an enormous number of small granules, very regular in size, form, and optical properties. They are almost perfectly spherical and are highly refractive, and possess a slightly yellowish tinge.

In many species these granules can be easily seen to be contained in the mesenchymatous cells, but here no evidence of cell structure in connection with them can be made out in most cases. It is probable that the cell substance has become wholly converted into the granules, though just how the thing is accomplished is not clear, since the bodies into which the granules are aggregated are much larger than the individual mesenchyme or body-substance cells ever are, and at the same time they appear to be too definite and constant in form to permit, without much misgiving, the supposition that they are formed from the running together of several cells. Their form approaches spherical in almost all cases where they are not under external pressure from some cause. Many of them reach a diameter of 45 or 50 μ, while their average size would probably be about 30 μ. From their form and behavior under pressure of the cover slip, and from what is known of the similar bodies in other species, it is quite certain that each one possesses an exceedingly thin membrane. But this is difficult to prove directly. In most, if not in all of these free post-abdomens portions of the mantle containing the characteristic muscle fibers and epithelial cells are present, and also the heart and the epicardiac tubes may frequently be found.

But the most interesting facts in connection with them relate to the sexual cells and their development. In many of the abdomens, particularly those that are least changed in form and structure, the band-shaped ovary is found to differ in no respect from the condition which it presents in ordinary normal zooids. (Fig. 28, *ov.*) The ova, however, many of them at least, are distinctly amoeboid, and at no period of their existence are they enveloped by either a follicular epithelium or "test" cells (Pl. LXXXVI, figs. 29, 29ª, 29ᵇ.) The absence of these two layers, the latter of which in particular is so characteristic of the tunicate ovum, is noteworthy. I know of no other instance of the kind in the group. This peculiarity of the individual ova gives an appearance to the ovary as a whole strikingly different from that of the ordinary ovary of these animals. The ova are very closely packed together, and the pseudopodia-like processes, in some instances quite long and narrow, lock together and overlap in an intricate way; and as the cytoplasm is quite homogeneous and refractile, particularly in the smaller and middle-sized ova, the appearance is, as remarked above, striking. Whether or not this amoeboid condition prevails before the abdomen is separated from the rest of the zooid, I do not know; but in all probability it does, since the smaller ova of the severed abdomens show it to almost as great a degree as do the larger ones. The character is, however, wholly lost before maturation takes place. At least this is the case so far as my observations have gone. I have found a few ova, one of which is shown in Pl. LXXXVI, fig. 30, that are perfectly spherical, and as the cytoplasm of these is entirely filled with food granules, I assume that they are nearly ready to undergo the maturation changes.

In addition to the amoeboid form of the ova, they show the same nature to a still greater extent in their *power of ingesting other cells*. Figs. 29 and 29ᵇ (Pl. LXXXVI) illustrate this. That the small cells are actually contained in the cytoplasm of the ova, and are not merely situated on the surface, may be shown conclusively by isolating the ova and so manipulating the cover slip as to cause them to swim about and turn over in the fluid in which they are contained. Such ova as the ones figured, showing the cells in various stages of penetration and disintegration, are very abundant. Ova are easily found in which as many as five or six of the ingested cells may be seen.

I have not been able to satisfy myself as to the nature of these cells. Such instances as that shown at *a*, fig. 29ᵇ, where the cell is only embedded in the surface of the ovum, gives rise to the suspicion that they represent either the follicular epithelial cells or the "test" cells, characteristic of the ova of tunicates. They may also, at least in some cases, be very young ova. Indeed it is highly probable that *many of the ova are consumed by their companions, for certain it is that only a small fraction of the entire number contained in an ovary ever develop into embryos*. I have said that the cytoplasm of the smaller and middle-sized ova is quite homogeneous and refractile, and also that in the older ones it is filled with food granules. These granules in such an ovum as the one shown in fig. 30, for example, are not recognizably different from those already described as constituting most of the bulk of the large bodies which I have said fill the post-abdomen, and which are in all probability yolk-laden mesenchyme cells.

There is little doubt that the yolk granules serve as nutriment for the growing ova and embryos, as do the ingested young ova and "test" cells (?). It is true I have not been able to actually observe the ingestion of the granules by the ova, but the fact that they have wholly disappeared from the cavities in which the embryos are situated by the time the fully developed tadpole stage is reached hardly admits of any other explanation. My failure to observe the ingestion of the granules by the growing ova may be due to the fact that the process actually does not begin until a comparatively late stage in the growth of the latter. If such be the case, it is probably due to the fact that the young ova and the "test" and follicular epithelial cells furnish a more accessible and an ample food supply for the ova during the early stages of their growth. This would result not only from the fact that the ova are held in the ovary for a time, but also from the further fact that the masses of yolk granules are, as already pointed out, enveloped by a membrane at the time when the post-abdomen is set free from the zooid.

It is worthy of special notice in this connection that at no time in the career of the growing ovarian ova are there, so far as my observations have gone, any indications of amoeboid or other changes in their nuclei. As is seen by reference to figure 30, Pl. LXXXVI, the germinative vesicle presents in each ovum the familiar characteristics of this body in ovarian ova, and this notwithstanding the fact that the ova are actively ingesting and presumably digesting also.

The embryonic stages which I have observed are the early cleavage stages (Pl. LXXXVI, fig. 31); late morula and early gastrula stages (fig. 32); fully developed tadpoles, and tadpoles in which the metamorphosis is well advanced (fig. 33). I describe the last two of these first. On making a section of the lobes of several of the colonies, packets of bodies, a few of which are shown in figure 27, are found embedded in the semi cartilaginous test. Cursory examination proves the bodies to be embryos in various stages of development. In one capsule, almost perfectly spherical, 3 mm. in diameter, were contained 13 embryos; in another, 3.5 mm. in diameter, were 16 embryos. Others examined contained fewer than the first mentioned, but none more than the last. The embryos are very closely packed together in the capsule, and they constitute its entire contents, so that after they are picked out the capsule is entirely empty and its interior is almost as regular and smooth as that of a bullet mold. The capsules are perfectly closed at all points. Concerning the embryos themselves, not much need be said. Figure 33 shows one in which the metamorphosis is well advanced.

The structural fact of most interest in connection with the full-grown embryos is the thickness and the composition of their own test. A general idea of this is given by figure 33 ts (Pl. LXXXVI), and a more detailed representation is shown by figure 34. The interest that attaches to this point lies in the probable fact that some of the elements contained in the test are unconsumed remnants of the extra ovarian portions of the post-abdomens of the parent zooids. There can be scarcely a doubt that such is the nature of the bodies shown at $y'k$, figure 34. These have the form, size, and composition of many of the masses of yolk granules already described as constituting so large a part of the bulk of the recently severed post-abdomen. In another part of the test of the same embryo there occurred a considerable number of fibers (Pl. LXXXVI, fig. 34 $m. f.$) which so strongly resembled the ordinary muscle fibers of the mantle of the adult that I should not have thought of questioning their nature but for the remarkable position occupied by them. Structures more or less similar both to the masses and the fibers are very common in almost every embryo. Most of these certainly belong to the test of the embryo itself, and are of course the same as those similarly situated in the embryos of all tunicates. But the number is here unusually large, and when this circumstance is considered along with that of the structure of the ones described above, it appears almost certain that, as already said, some of the various bodies contained in the test of the embryos are remnants of the parent zooids. Whether or not this would signify that the test of the embryo serves in any way as a medium of nutrition I do not know. The mere fact of the presence in the test of parental substance that might be used for food by the embryo would not prove that it actually is so used. Both the fibers and the bodies which I have described and figured are, as a matter of fact, either imbedded in or only slightly beneath the surface of the embryonic test, and their presence there may signify no more, so far as the nutrition of the embryo is concerned, than do the great variety of foreign bodies that may be found imbedded in the test of almost all tunicates. Nevertheless, the facts as presented do undoubtedly raise this very interesting question, and there is certainly some ground for suspecting that the test in these embryos does actually play a part in the nutritive function.

All the developmental stages that I have found earlier than the tadpole were contained in a single post-abdomen. This had evidently been quite recently set free from the zooid, since it still retained nearly its usual form and size. It was 4 mm. long and quite narrow as compared with the almost perfectly spherical shape assumed at a later time.

It only remains to say a few words about the fertilization of the ova. I have found fully developed spermatozoa in several post-abdomens, but not in any of those containing embryos. I have, however, seen so few post-abdomens with embryos in the early stages of development that I would not venture to conclude that the same individuals never do contain both ripe sperm and ova at the same time, and hence that self-fertilization does not take place. In fact it appears exceedingly probable that this is the method of fertilization. Certain it is that ripe sperm and well-developed ovarian ova occur together in the same abdomen, and it is difficult to conceive either that self-fertilization would be avoided in such cases, or how it could be accomplished in any other way after the post-abdomens have become set free and fully and deeply imbedded, as they do, in the hard test of the colony.

In conclusion, I must express my regrets that I have not sufficient material to make possible a fuller account of the interesting processes here seen in outline only. The facts are sufficient, however, to render this outline quite distinct, and we may hope that opportunity will come before many years to fill in more of the details.

BERKELEY, *February 17, 1898.*

EXPLANATION OF FIGURES.

Fig. 1. *Dendrodoa tuberculata*, natural size.
Fig. 2. The branchial and atrial orifices of *D. tuberculata*, with their adjacent parts, seen from the inside.
Fig. 3. The left half of the branchial sac of *D. tuberculata*, seen from the inside.
Fig. 4. Small portion of the branchial sac of *D. tuberculata*, from the inside.
Fig. 5. The ovary, in place on the mantle, of *D. tuberculata*.
Fig. 6. General view of *D. subpedunculata*, natural size.
Fig. 7. A group of eleven individuals of *D. subpedunculata* attached to a fragment of seaweed. Two of these fused together.
Fig. 8. Specimen of *D. tuberculata* dissected to show the digestive tract and ovary in outline. The bands at *x*, and having considerable resemblance to the ovary, are folds in the mantle. (See note under description of species in the text relating to position of parts in this figure.)
Figs. 9 and 10. *Styela greeleyi*.
Fig. 11. Branchial sac of *S. greeleyi*.
Fig. 12. Digestive tract and sexual organs of same species.

Fig. 13. Branchial tentacles of same.

Fig. 14. Colony of *Polyclinum globosum*, with a portion cut away. The small area at β indicates about the distribution of the zooids, and shows the branchial orifices, though much more distinctly than they can actually be seen.

Fig. 15. A single zooid of same species.

Fig. 16. Atrial languet of same, seen from the under side.

Figs. 17A and 17B. Two sectioned colonies of *Polyclinum pannosum*, 17A showing the zooids in their normal form and position, and 17B the degenerated zooids. The characteristic ragged surface of the colony is shown at y, 17B.

Fig. 18. Portion of a zooid of *P. pannosum*.

Fig. 19. A colony of *Aplidiopsis jordani* with an individual of *Dendrodoa subpedunculata*, D. S., imbedded in it.

Fig. 20. A zooid of *A. jordani*. The post-abdomen outlined in this specimen is unusually short.

Figs. 21, 21A, and 21B. Portions of different zooids of *Amaroucium kincaidi*. 21A and 21B drawn particularly to show the equivocal character of the irregularities in the stomach walls.

Fig. 22. A colony of *Amaroucium snodgrassi*. The specimen is seen from its base, B, and one of its precipitous edges, on which latter the zooids z are visible through the semitransparent test.

Fig. 23. Stomach and small portion of intestinal loop of *Amaroucium snodgrassi*.

Fig. 23A. Anterior end of zooid of same species, seen from inside.

Fig. 23B. A few of the remarkably long, narrow stigmata of same species.

Fig. 24. A colony of *Amaroucium pribilovense*.

Fig. 25. A single zooid, the posterior part of the post-abdomen wanting, of the same species.

Fig. 26. A colony of *Synoicum irregulare*.

Fig. 27. The cut surface of one of the lobes of a colony of same species, showing the packages of embryos, e, imbedded in the test.

Fig. 28. A zooid of *S. irregulare*.

Plate LXXXVI.

Figs. 29, 29a, and 29b. Ovarian ova of *S. irregulare*, 29 and 29b containing ingested cells. × 360.

Fig. 30. An ovarian ovum, presumably nearly ready for maturation. × 360.

Fig. 31. Two-celled stage. × 360.

Fig. 32. Morula? early gastrula stage. × 360.

Fig. 33. Embryo well advanced in metamorphosis. This from one of the cavities containing embryos only. × 40.

Fig. 34. Small portion of the test of an old embryo. The cellular masses, x, are the same as the bodies shown at x, fig. 33. These probably belong to the test of the embryo itself. The mass y. k. is imbedded in the test, and is without doubt a cluster of the mesenchymatous yolk containing bodies found in the parental post-abdomen. m. f. appear to be muscle fibers derived from the mantle of the parent.

BIBLIOGRAPHY.

BONNEVIE, KRISTINE.
    1896. Ascidiae Simplices og Ascidiae Compositae. Den Norske Nordhavs-Expedition, 1876–1878. XXIII, Zoologi.

EDWARDS, MILNE.
    1846. Observations sur les ascidies composées des Côtes de la Manche. Mémoires de l'Académie royale des sciences de l'Institute de France. T. XVIII, 1846.

GIARD, A.
    1872. Recherches sur les Ascidies composées, ou Synascidies. Thèses, 1872.

HANCOCK, ALBANY.
    1868. On the Anatomy and Physiology of the Tunicata. Journal Linnean Society—Zoology. Vol. IX, 1868.

HELLER, CAUSIL.
    1877. Untersuchungen über die Tunicaten des Adriatischen und Mittelmeeres. III (1) Abtheilung. Denkschriften d. kais. Akad. d. Wissensch. Wien, Math.-naturwiss. Classe. Bd. XXXVII, 1877.

HERDMAN, W. A.
  1882. Report on the Tunicata collected during the voyage of H. M. S. *Challenger* during the years 1873–1876. Challenger Reports, Zoology, Vol. VI, 1882.
  1886. Report on the Tunicata. Challenger Expedition, Part II. Ascidiae Compositae, 1886.
  1891. A Revised Classification of the Tunicata, with Definitions of the Orders, Suborders, Families, Subfamilies, and Genera and Analytical Keys to the Species. Linnean Society's Journal—Zoology. Vol. XXIII, 1891.

HUITFELDT-KAAS, H.
  1896. Synascidiae. Den Norske Nordhavs-Expedition, 1876–1878, XXIII, Zoologi.

KIÆR, JOHN.
  1893. Oversigt over Norges Ascidiæ simplices. Christiania Videnskabs-Selskabs Forhandlinger, No. 9.

LAHILLE, F.
  1890. Contributions a l'étude anatomique et taxonomique des Tuniciers. Thèses, 1890.

MACLEAY, WILLIAM S.
  1824. Anatomical Observations on the Natural Group of Tunicata, with Descriptions of three Species Collected in Fox Channel During the late Northern Expedition. Linnean Society Transactions, Vol. XIV, 1824.

SAVIGNY, JULES-CÉSAR.
  1816. Mémoir sur les Animaux sans Vertèbres. 2d Partie, 1816.

TRAUSTEDT, M. P. A.
  1882. Die einfachen Ascidien (Ascidiae simplices) des Golfes von Neapel. Mittheil. a. d. Zoolog. Station zu Neapel. IV Bd. 4 Hft.

ABBREVIATIONS USED IN THE ILLUSTRATIONS.

A	Anterior, or siphonal end.
B	Base, or posterior end.
a. l	Atrial languet.
a. o	Atrial orifice.
a. t	Atrial tentacles.
b. f	Branchial folds.
b. s	Branchial stigmata.
br. s	Branchial sac.
br. si	Branchial siphon.
b. t	Branchial tentacles.
d. l	Dorsal lamina.
d. t	Dorsal tubercle.
emb	Embryo.
en'c	"Endocarps."
ep	Epicardiac tubes.
h	Heart.
i. l. v	Internal longitudinal vessels.
m. c. v	Muscle bands of circular vessels.
o. œ	Œsophageal mouth.
o. p	Optic pigment.
œ	Œsophagus.
ov	Ovary.
p. b	Peribranchial band.
r	Rectum.
st	Stomach.
t	Testis.
t_1, t_2, t_3, t_4	Transverse vessels of different orders.
ts	Test, or cellulose "mantle."
v. d	Vas deferens.
y'k	Yolk-containing mesenchyme cells.
z	Zooid.

PLATE LXXXVI.

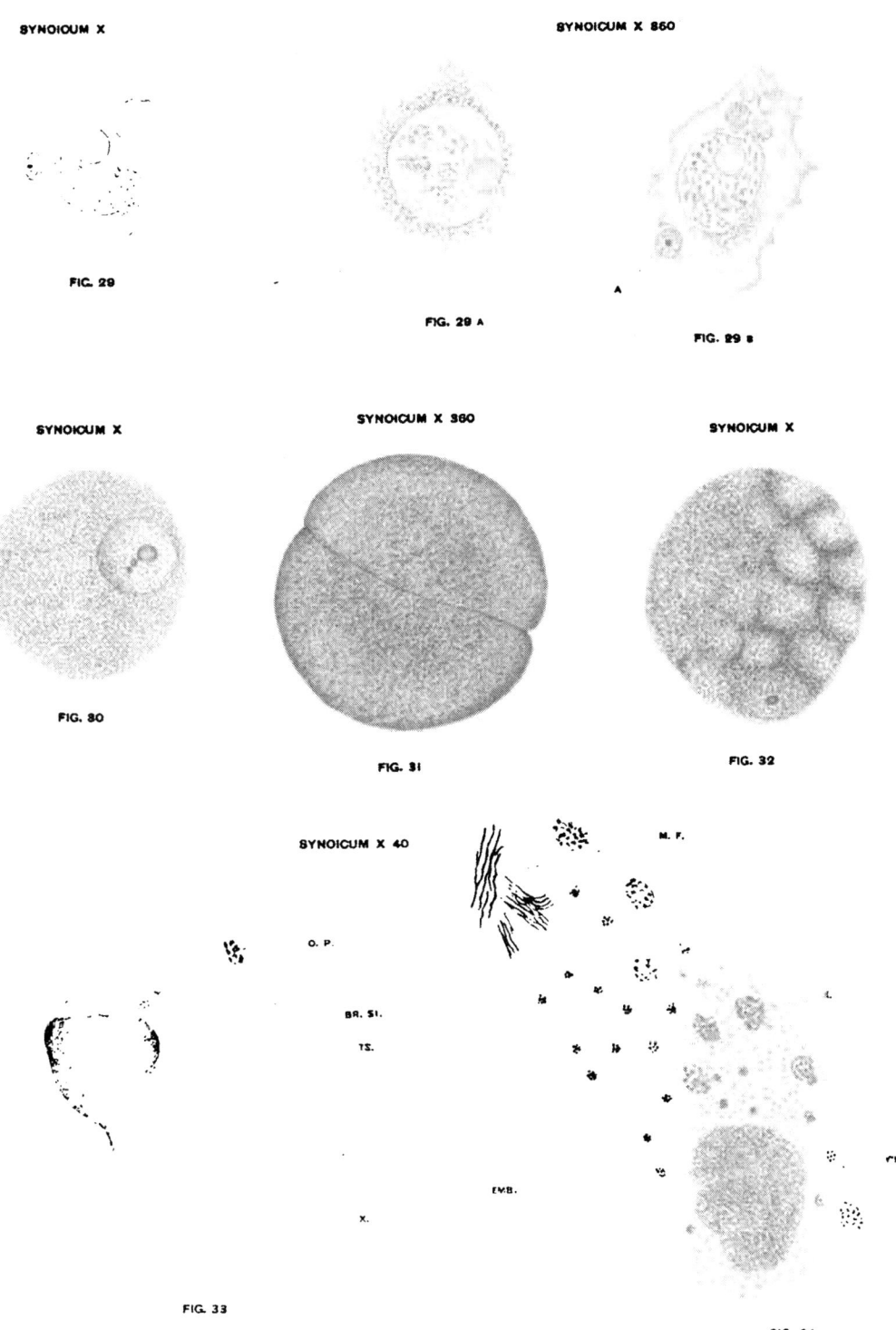

DEVELOPMENT OF SYNOICUM IRREGULARE.

Printed by Libri Plureos GmbH in Hamburg, Germany